Science Matters
PLANETS

Michelle Lomberg

WEIGL PUBLISHERS INC.

Published by Weigl Publishers Inc.
123 South Broad Street, Box 227
Mankato, MN USA 56002
Web site: www.weigl.com

Library of Congress Cataloging-in-Publication Data

Lomberg, Michelle.
  Planets / Michelle Lomberg.
      v. cm. -- (Science matters)
Includes index.
Contents: Getting to know planets -- Planets in the past -- Planet parts
-- Planets on the move -- Map of our solar system -- Planet people --
Planetary probes -- Peeking at planets -- Surfing our solar system --
Science in action -- What have you learned?
  ISBN 1-59036-086-9 (lib. bdg. : alk. paper)
 1. Planets--Juvenile literature. [1. Planets.] I. Title. II. Series.
  QB602 .L66 2003
  523.4--dc21

                          2002013853

Printed in the United States of America
1 2 3 4 5 6 7 8 9 0 06 05 04 03 02

Project Coordinator Jennifer Nault **Design** Terry Paulhus
Copy Editor Nicole Bezic King **Layout** Bryan Pezzi **Photo Researcher** Tina Schwartzenberger

Photograph Credits
Every reasonable effort has been made to trace ownership and to obtain permission to reprint copyright material. The publishers would be pleased to have any errors or omissions brought to their attention so that they may be corrected in subsequent printings.

Cover: Saturn from Digital Vision
Bettmann/CORBIS/MAGMA: page 15; Warren Clark: pages 11, 12-13; COMSTOCK, Inc.: pages 3B, 14, 19; Corel Corporation: pages 3T, 23T; Digital Vision: title page, pages 3M, 4, 6, 8, 10, 21, 22T, 23M, 23B; NASA: page 18; NASA/NSSDC: page 16; PhotoDisc, Inc.: page 22B.

Contents

Studying Planets

Much can be seen in the sky on a clear night. Some objects in space pass by the twinkling stars and slowly travel across the sky. Moving space objects are usually planets. The word planet comes from the Greek word *planete*, which means "wanderer."

Earth is one of the nine planets in our **solar system**. All of the planets travel around the Sun. The nine planets are Mercury, Venus, Earth, Mars, Jupiter, Saturn, Uranus, Neptune, and Pluto.

■ There are many more planets in the universe than the nine planets of our solar system.

Planet Facts

Did you know that Earth is the only planet known to support life in our solar system? There are many other interesting facts about the nine planets.

- Mercury is the closest planet to the Sun.

- Venus is the brightest planet.

- Earth is the **densest** space object in our solar system.

- Mars is the second-closest planet to Earth.

- Jupiter is the largest planet.

- Saturn is known for its colorful rings.

- Uranus has rings and spins on its side.

- Neptune is surrounded by thick gases.

- Pluto is the smallest planet.

Planets in the Past

The ancient Aztec peoples watched and studied the planets. They prayed to the objects they saw in the sky as gods. Venus was the most important planet for the Aztecs. The planet Venus represented the god *Tlahuizcalpantecuhtli*. This long name means "Lord of the House of Dawn."

■ The Aztecs held festivals for the planet Venus at certain times of the year.

Planet Names

The name *Earth* comes from an English word that means "ground" or "soil." The other planets are named after Roman or Greek gods.

MERCURY messenger god

VENUS goddess of love and beauty

EARTH ground or soil

MARS god of war

JUPITER king of the gods

SATURN god of farming

URANUS god of the sky

NEPTUNE god of the sea

PLUTO god of the **underworld**

Planet Parts

Earth, Mars, Mercury, and Venus are called **terrestrial** planets. They consist mainly of rock. Some of these planets have a thin **atmosphere**. Others have no atmosphere.

Jupiter, Neptune, Saturn, and Uranus are made up mostly of gas. They are called gas giants. The atmospheres of these planets are thousands of miles thick.

Pluto is made up of ice and rock. Its atmosphere is lost as quickly as it is created.

■ Earth's atmosphere is mostly made up of gases.

Planet Sizes

The nine planets are different sizes. Jupiter is the largest planet in our solar system. Pluto is smaller than Earth's moon.

A diameter is a measurement of a circle. It measures a straight line passing through the center of a circle, from one side to the other. The nine planets each have different diameter lengths.

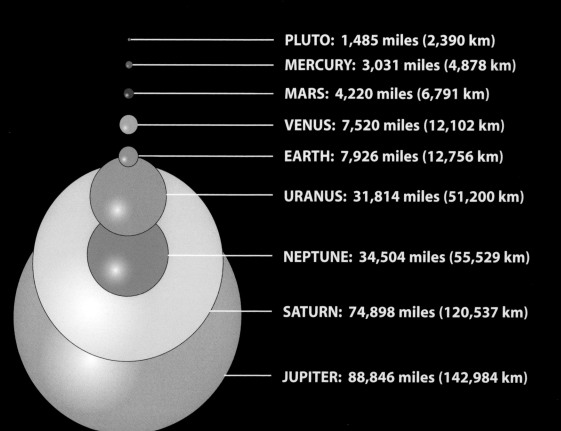

PLUTO: 1,485 miles (2,390 km)

MERCURY: 3,031 miles (4,878 km)

MARS: 4,220 miles (6,791 km)

VENUS: 7,520 miles (12,102 km)

EARTH: 7,926 miles (12,756 km)

URANUS: 31,814 miles (51,200 km)

NEPTUNE: 34,504 miles (55,529 km)

SATURN: 74,898 miles (120,537 km)

JUPITER: 88,846 miles (142,984 km)

Planets on the Move

The nearly circular path that a planet makes around the Sun is called an **orbit**. All planets travel **counterclockwise**. Most planets' orbits are elliptical. This means that they are not quite perfect circles.

The time that it takes a planet to complete a full orbit is the length of its year. Mercury takes only 88 Earth days to travel around the Sun. One year on Mars is almost as long as 2 Earth years. It takes 248 Earth years to equal 1 year on Pluto.

■ The force that keeps the planets in our solar system orbiting the Sun is called gravity.

Spinning in Space

Did you know that the planets spin? While each planet orbits the Sun, it also spins like a top.

The time that it takes a planet to spin around once is the length of its day. Earth takes 24 hours to spin around once. One day on Earth is 24 hours long. Saturn takes only 11 hours to complete one spin.

Earth takes 365 days to orbit the Sun. The seasons change according to the position of Earth in its orbit.

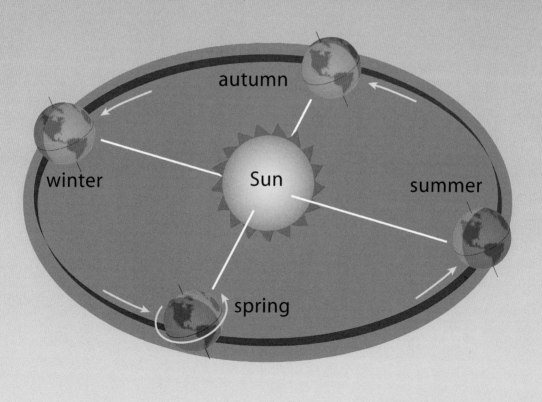

autumn

winter

Sun

summer

spring

Solar System Map

Match each planet on the left to its orbit in the diagram. This will show you the order of the planets in our solar system.

- Mercury

- Venus

- Earth

- Mars

- Jupiter

- Saturn

- Uranus

- Neptune

- Pluto

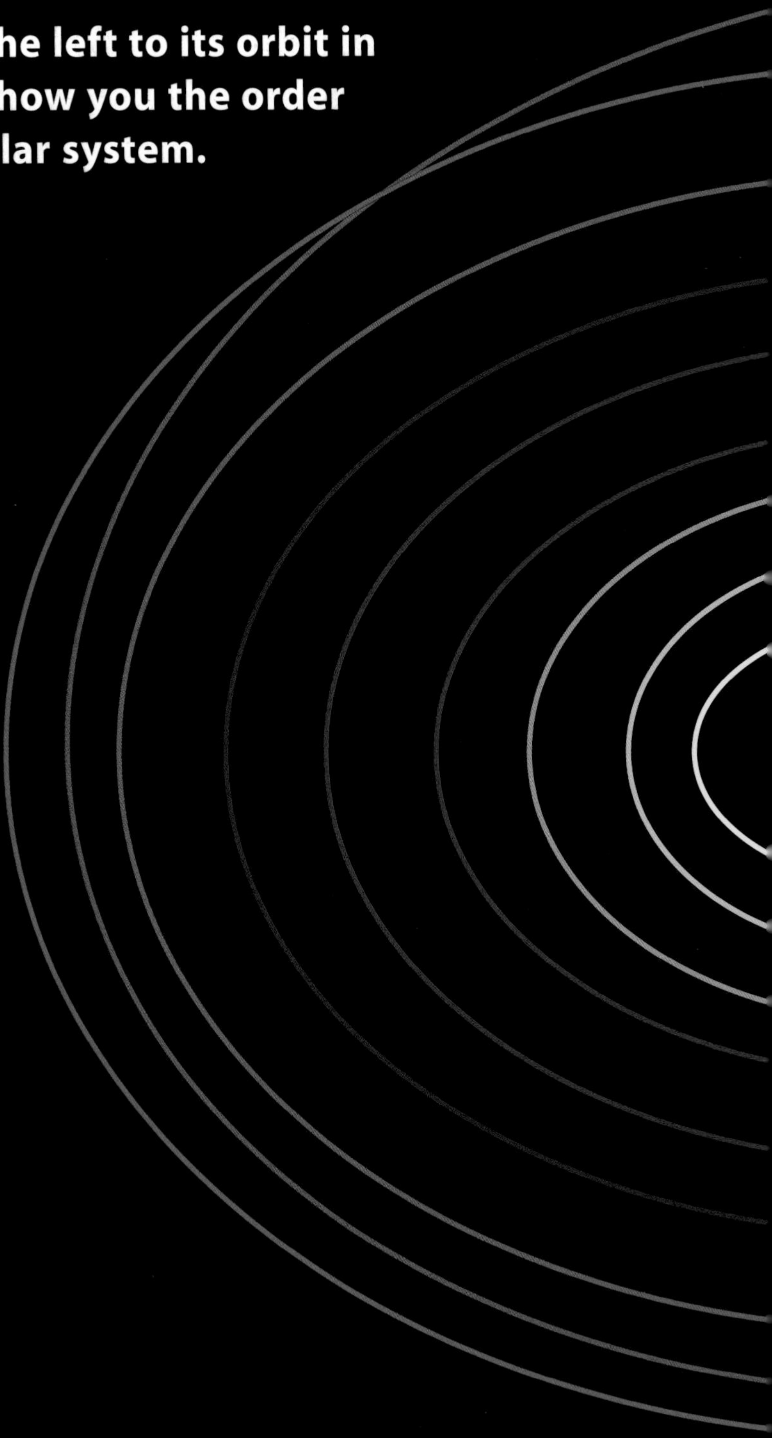

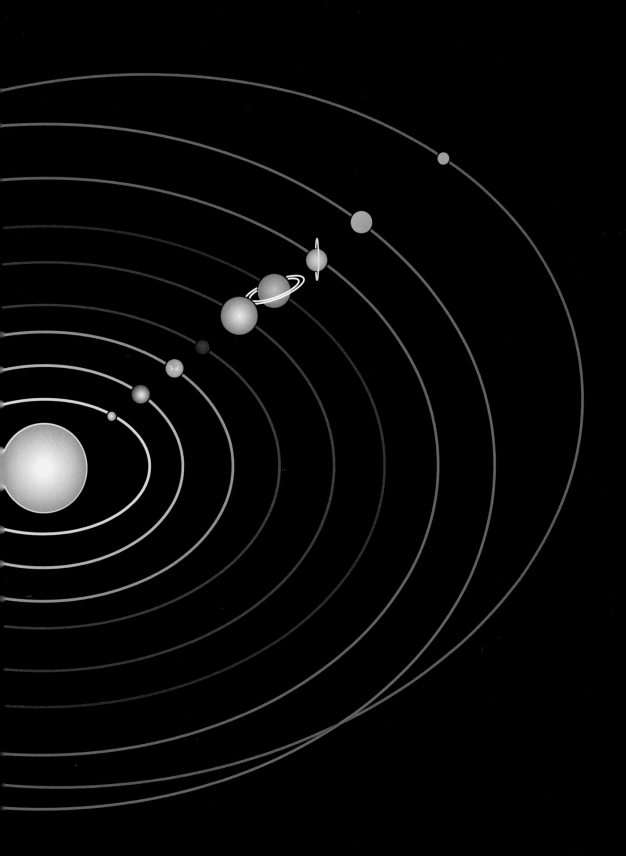

Planet People

Astronomers study planets and other objects in space. Astronomy is the study of planets, stars, and other space objects. Astronomers use powerful **telescopes** to gather information about planets. Astronomers usually do not look through the telescopes. Instead, the telescopes send information to computers. Astronomers are trained to understand the information gathered by telescopes.

■ Astronomers use radio telescopes to learn about our solar system.

A Life of Science

Percival Lowell

Percival Lowell was an astronomer from Boston, Massachusetts. When Percival began studying planets, Pluto had not yet been discovered. Percival believed that a ninth planet existed. Percival studied the planets at an **observatory** in Flagstaff, Arizona. His careful research helped another astronomer discover Pluto. Percival's work led to Clyde William Tombaugh's discovery of Pluto, in 1930.

Planet Probes

Humans have never set foot on any planet other than Earth. Astronomers collect information about planets by sending probes into space. Space probes are spacecrafts that are controlled from Earth. They can take photographs, measure temperatures, and collect rocks and dirt. Space probes have gathered information about all the planets except Pluto.

■ A space probe that touches down on the surface of a planet is called a lander.

Many Moons

Astronauts have not yet traveled to other planets. They have visited Earth's moon. Many planets have their own moons, too.

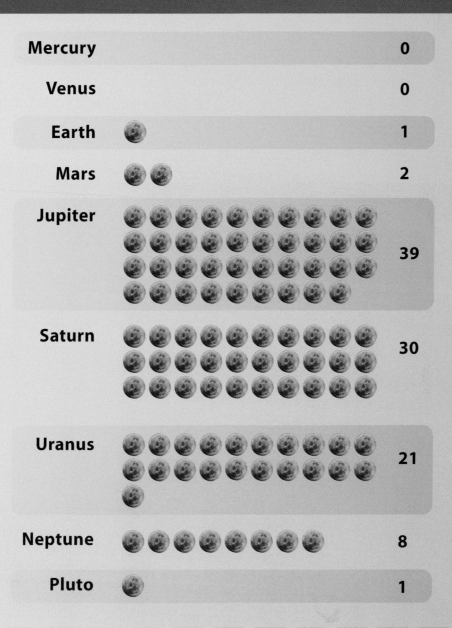

Mercury	0
Venus	0
Earth	1
Mars	2
Jupiter	39
Saturn	30
Uranus	21
Neptune	8
Pluto	1

Peeking at Planets

Computer and space probes are not necessary to observe the planets. They can see some of the planets can be seen with their own eyes.

Planets look like stars, but they do not twinkle. Venus is brighter than most stars. It is often the first object that can be seen in the evening sky. When Mars is close to Earth, it looks like a bright, red star. Jupiter's moons and Saturn's rings can be seen with a small telescope.

■ Venus and Mars look like stars in the early morning sky.

Planet Puzzler

Does Saturn have ears?

Planets look like bright, blurry stars without a telescope. In 1610, an Italian astronomer named Galileo Galilei was the first person to point his telescope at the night sky. When he looked at Saturn, he was surprised. It looked like the planet had ears.

What did Galileo see?

Answer: Saturn's rings

Surfing Our Solar System

How can I find more information about space?
- Libraries have many interesting books about space.
- Science centers are great places to learn about space.
- The Internet offers some great Web sites dedicated to space.

Where can I find a good reference Web site to learn more about space?
Encarta Homepage
www.encarta.com
- Type any space-related term into the search engine. Some terms to try include "asteroid" and "galaxy."

How can I find out more about space, rockets, and astronauts?
NASA Kids
http://kids.msfc.nasa.gov
- This Web site offers puzzles and games, along with the latest news on NASA's research.

Science in Action

Space Vacation

Find information on your favorite planet. Research its color, temperature, weather, moons, and other details. On one side of a piece of construction paper, draw and color a picture of the planet. On the other side, write a postcard describing your imaginary vacation on the planet.

Look Up!

Look up at the sky just after sunset or before sunrise. Can you spot a low, bright star that does not twinkle? That star is probably the planet Venus.

What Have You Learned?

1 Which planet is known for its rings?

2 Which planet is closest to the Sun?

3 Which planet is the smallest?

4 What does the word *planet* mean?

5 How do most large telescopes collect information?

6 What are planets made of?

7 Which planet in our solar system has the most moons?

8 Which four planets are known as the gas giants?

9 Which is the brightest planet in the sky?

10 On which planet is human life found?

Answers: 1. Saturn **2.** Mercury **3.** Pluto **4.** *Planet* means "wanderer" **5.** Most large telescopes send information directly to computers. **6.** Rock, gas, and ice **7.** Jupiter, with thirty-nine known moons **8.** Jupiter, Saturn, Uranus, and Neptune **9.** Venus **10.** Earth

Words to Know

atmosphere: the layer of gases surrounding a planet

counterclockwise: the direction opposite to the movement of the hands of a clock

densest: packed closely together

observatory: a building consisting of a large telescope

orbit: the nearly circular path a planet makes around an object in the sky, such as the Sun

solar system: the Sun, the planets, and other objects that move around the Sun

telescopes: an instrument that makes distant objects appear closer

terrestrial: related to Earth

underworld: in Greek stories, the place where the souls of the dead go

Index

Fun with

Shapes

M

THE MILLBROOK PRESS

Brookfield, Connecticut

Published in the United States in 1998 by

M

The Millbrook Press, Inc.
2 Old New Milford Road
Brookfield, Connecticut 06804

First published in the UK in 1998 by

Belitha Press Limited
London House, Great Eastern Wharf
Parkgate Road, London SW11 4NQ

Series editor: Honor Head
Series designer: Jamie Asher
Illustrator: Brigitte McDonald
U.S. Math Consultant: Henrietta Pesce

Patilla, Peter.
Fun with shapes/written by Peter Patilla; illustrated by
Brigitte McDonald.
p.   cm.
Summary: Uses a variety of picture puzzles to teach
the basic geometric concept of shape.
ISBN 0-7613-0958-6 (lib. bdg.)
1. Geometry–Juvenile literature. 2. Mathematical
recreations–Juvenile literature. 3. Picture puzzles–
Juvenile literature. [1. Geometry. 2. Shape 3. Picture
puzzles.] I. McDonald, Brigitte, ill. II. Title.
QA445.5.P38 1998
516–dc21
98–16665
CIP AC

Printed in Hong Kong

Fun with

Shapes

written by
Peter Patilla

illustrated by
Brigitte McDonald

About This Series

The four books in this series, *Fun With Numbers, Fun With Shapes, Fun With Sizes,* and *Fun With Patterns,* provide an engaging format to explore beginning mathematical concepts with children. They may investigate the books on their own, but extending this investigation with an adult will bring added value to the experience. The following suggestions are provided as a guide for you to help your child or students get the most from the series.

Fun With Shapes

The function of shape impacts how comfortably we live. For example, what would the world be like without the discovery of the wheel? Realizing that each shape has distinctive properties is an important learning step for a young child. Asking questions like, "Would a bicycle move faster if it had a different shape?" will bring into focus the importance of shape in everyday experiences. In this book, children will look at shapes from different perspectives, learning that although the view changes, the shape remains the same.

They will also compare and match shapes, discussing likeness and difference.

Before opening *Fun With Shapes*, talk about the word "shape." What does it mean? What kind of shapes can be found on the cover of the book? Ask children to describe these various shapes. Talk about what it would be like to ride a bike with square wheels, or fly a plane with round wings. Hide part of a shape (one side of a triangle, for example) and ask the children if they can name the shape. Encourage them to use specific language when they talk about shapes, especially solid shapes. As you explore the puzzles and games in *Fun With Shapes*, use these ideas to add to the mathematical journey you are about to begin.

A Step Beyond

After you have finished exploring the book, go beyond these pages. Invite children to go on a junk hunt for shapes. Have them collect various three-dimensional items and build a geometric creation with the shapes. When they have finished, display the artwork and encourage children to describe what they have created. Don't put the book away—children will want to open *Fun With Shapes* again and again.

Mystery Gifts

These presents have been wrapped up.
Can you name them?

Can you find the teddy bear?
Can you find the airplane?
Can you find the bucket?

Viewpoints

Name these objects. Can you find them in the big picture?

9

Spot the Difference

Look at the house in these pictures.

Can you spot 8 differences?

Top to Bottom

Look at the shapes, sizes, and patterns of these boxes. Can you match the tops to the bottoms?

13

Feast of Fun

Find the odd shape on each plate.
Why is it different?

Sky Gazing

How many of these shapes can you find in the picture?

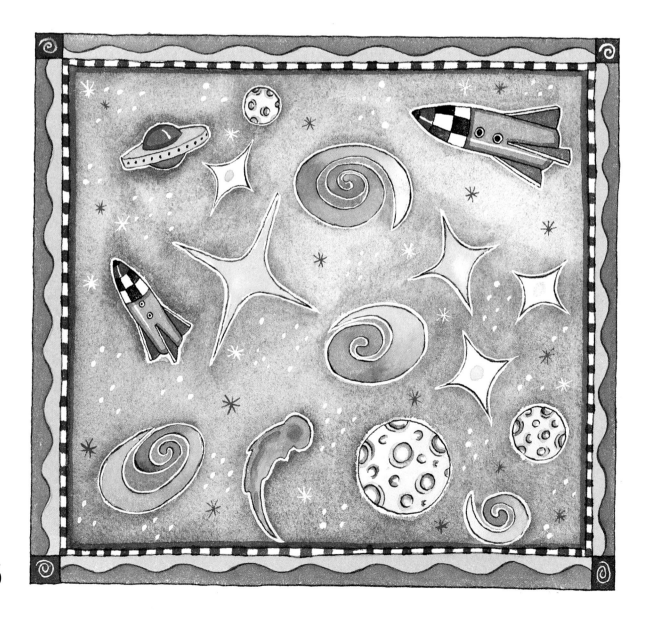

How many of these shapes can you find?

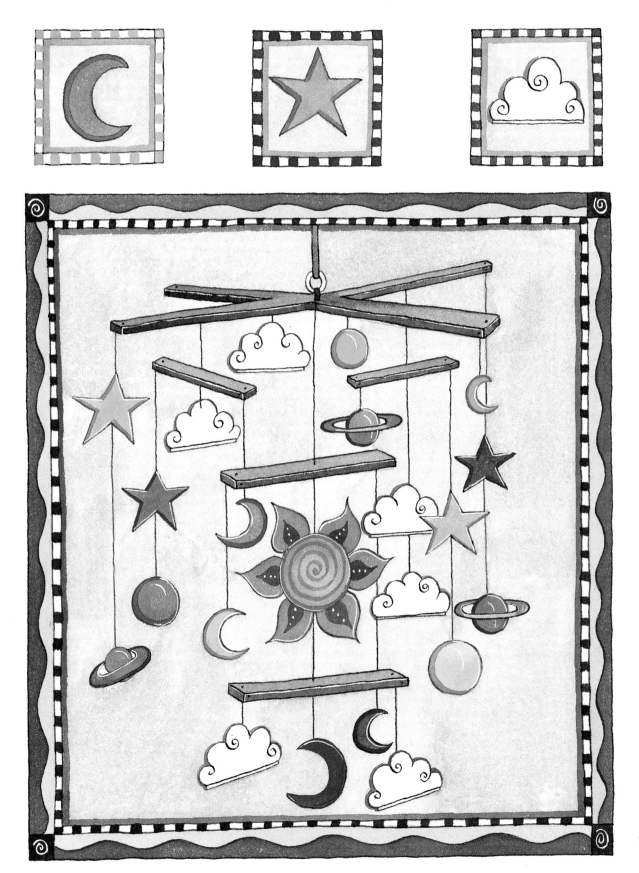

Set and Match

Find a set of three cards with the
same shape on the opposite page
and match it with a shape below.

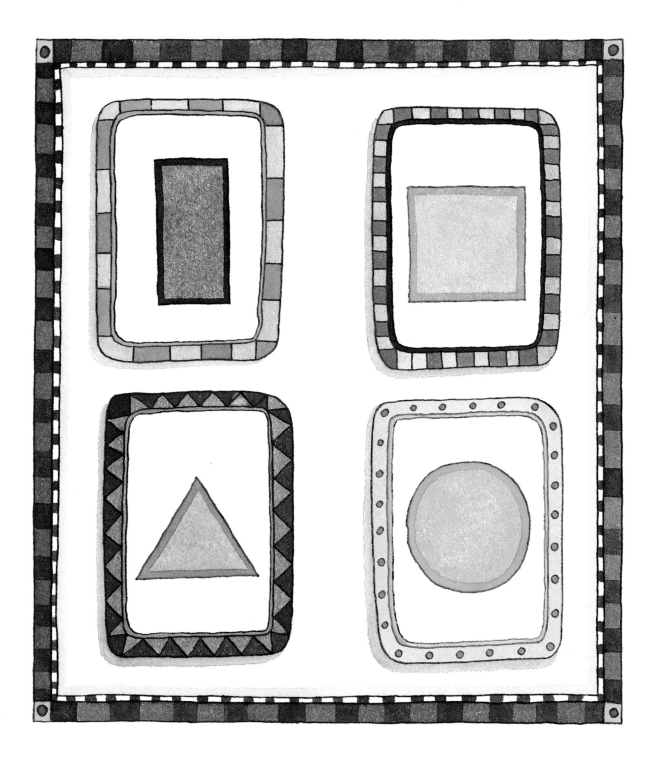

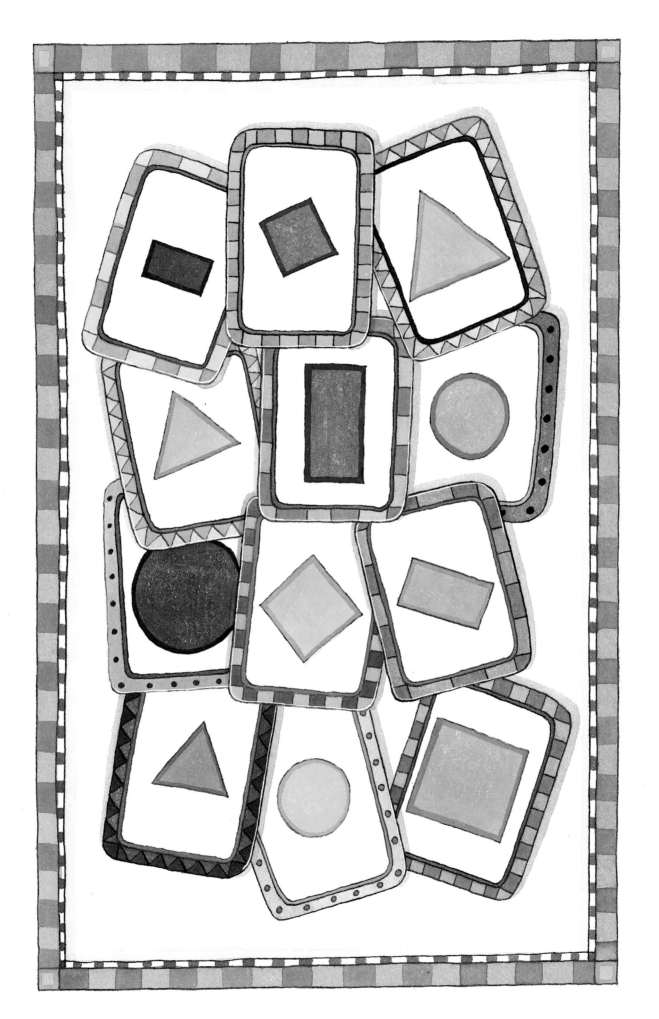

Shape Spotting

How many of these shapes can you find in the pictures?

21

Amazing Shapes

Match the shapes at the end of each path by following the same shapes through the maze.

Match the Shapes

Where does each shape fit?

Pipework

How many of these shapes can you see in the pipes below?

square

rectangle

circle

triangle

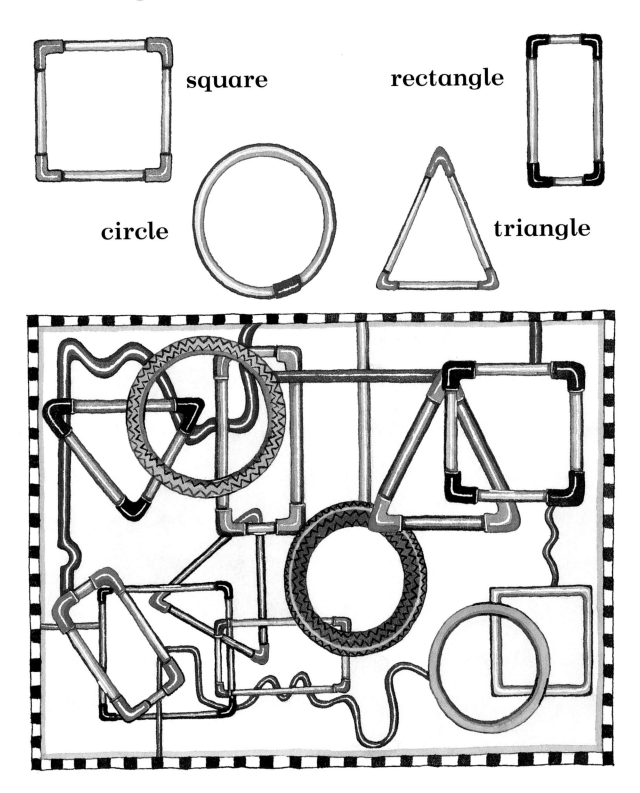

Shape Snap

Choose a shape below. Find a matching card and say "snap!"

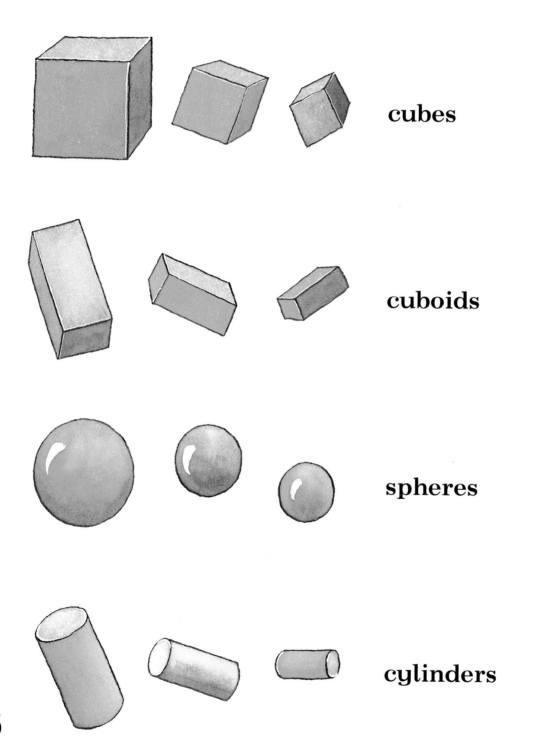

cubes

cuboids

spheres

cylinders

Up and Away

Can you find the shapes below in the picture?

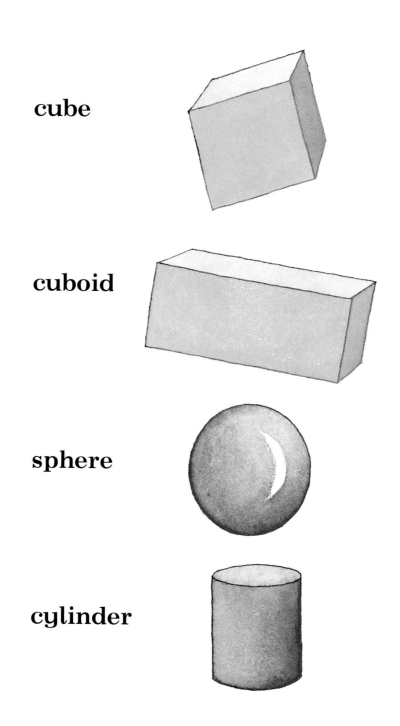

cube

cuboid

sphere

cylinder

Truck Loads

Can you find the odd shape in each truckload? What is each different shape called?

Shapes

square

circle

triangle

rectangle

cube

sphere

cylinder

cuboid